EMBRACING HUMANITY

A Call to Abandon Cultural Divisions and Unite as a Global Community

Introduction: A Call to Transcend Culture for the Survival of Humanity

For centuries, humanity has divided itself along lines that seem insurmountable—race, religion, ethnicity, and nationality. These divisions have fuelled countless wars, conflicts, and genocides. They have wasted untold resources and inflicted suffering on millions of people. From the Crusades to the Israeli-Palestinian conflict, from the Rwandan Genocide to the wars of Yugoslavia, history bears witness to the destruction caused by our inability to see past cultural differences. We continue to define ourselves by the narrow boundaries of ethnicity, colour, or faith—by identities that separate rather than unite us.

But this division is not only senseless; it's dangerous. Today, we stand at the edge of a precipice. The survival of our species is at risk, not just from the wars and conflicts that have always plagued us, but from global challenges like climate change, pandemics, and resource scarcity—problems that no single nation or culture can solve alone.

We can no longer afford to view the world through the narrow lens of cultural identity. The time has come for us to embrace something much greater: our shared **human identity**.

What does it mean to be human? It means that despite our superficial differences, we are fundamentally the same. We share 99.9% of the same DNA. We have the same needs for survival—food, water, shelter, and companionship. We share the same aspirations for peace, prosperity, and a better future for our children. And most importantly, we all face the same existential threats to our collective survival.

This book is a call to action. It is a call to let go of the divisions that have held us back for so long. It is a call to embrace a new identity—one based not on race, nationality, or religion, but on our common humanity. A human identity that transcends borders, breaks down walls, and fosters a world united by shared goals and collective responsibility. But this vision will not become reality on its own.

The world will not change unless we—everyday people—take action. It is the grassroots, the ordinary citizens, who must embrace this idea of **global citizenship** and push for leaders who share this vision. It is the people who must demand a new world order, one that sees beyond the divisions of culture and ethnicity to focus on the survival and flourishing of our species as a whole.

If we fail to take up this challenge—if we continue to cling to the identities that have caused so much harm—our future will be one of relentless conflict, environmental devastation, and, ultimately, collapse. The signs are already here, scattered across our history and our present, warning us of the path we are on.

A Future of Continued Conflict

If we persist in defining ourselves by our differences —by race, nationality, religion, or ethnicity—the divisions between us will continue to widen. We will remain locked in a cycle of misunderstanding and distrust, where nations compete for dominance and resources rather than collaborate for the common good. Borders will continue to harden, migration will be seen as a threat, and the rise of nationalism will fuel xenophobia and division.

Example: In such a future, we may see more conflicts erupt like those that have scarred our history— the wars in the Middle East, the ethnic cleansing in Rwanda, the partition of India and Pakistan.

Nationalism and cultural superiority will fuel new conflicts over dwindling resources like water, food, and arable land. Countries will invest more in militarization, building walls and stockpiling weapons, preparing for the inevitable clashes that arise when borders are closed and people are pitted against one another. Wars fought over ethnic or national identities will seem even more absurd and senseless in a world facing the shared threats of climate change and resource scarcity, but they will persist if we fail to embrace a global human identity.

Environmental Devastation

Even more pressing is the environmental catastrophe that looms ahead. If we fail to take up this challenge, if we continue to let national and corporate interests prioritize short-term gain over long-term sustainability, the impact on the planet will be devastating. Climate change, driven by unchecked industrial activity, deforestation, and the burning of fossil fuels, will accelerate beyond our control. Rising sea levels will swallow coastal cities, forcing mass migrations and displacing millions of people. Extreme weather events—hurricanes, droughts, wildfires—will become more frequent and more destructive.

Example: Imagine a world where vast regions of the planet become uninhabitable. Entire nations in the Pacific, such as Tuvalu or the Maldives, may be submerged beneath rising oceans. Countries like Bangladesh could face massive humanitarian crises as millions of people flee their flooded homes. Droughts will devastate crops, leading to food shortages and skyrocketing prices, triggering conflicts over water and arable land. The Amazon rainforest, once the lungs of the Earth, could be reduced to a barren wasteland, releasing more carbon into the atmosphere and exacerbating the climate crisis.

Without global cooperation, the situation will spiral out of control. Nations that fail to see beyond their borders will continue to act in their own short-term interests, refusing to cut emissions or share resources. The world will descend into chaos as we fight over the remnants of what was once a thriving planet. And as we face the consequences of our inaction, it will become clear that the divisions we clung to—our cultural and national identities—were trivial compared to the magnitude of the problems that now threaten our survival.

Economic Collapse and Inequality

The economic inequality that plagues the world today will only deepen if we continue down this path. The wealth gap will widen, with the richest few continuing to amass more power and resources, while billions remain trapped in poverty. Nations will compete in a race to the bottom, exploiting labor, hoarding wealth, and neglecting the welfare of their citizens in pursuit of dominance on the global stage.

Example: In such a world, the collapse of entire economies is not unthinkable. Global markets, already unstable due to resource scarcity and environmental degradation, will teeter on the brink of collapse as supply chains break down and consumer demand dwindles. Developing nations will suffer the most, facing famine, drought, and the devastation of their agricultural industries. Wealthier nations may attempt to shield themselves, but the interconnected nature of the global economy means that no country will be immune to the economic fallout. Trade wars, protectionist policies, and the collapse of international cooperation will make recovery nearly impossible.

The stark inequality between rich and poor will fuel unrest and revolution. People, tired of being left behind, will take to the streets, protesting the injustice of a system that prioritizes profit over human life. But without a unifying vision of global citizenship, these protests will devolve into chaos, with different groups fighting for power and resources, rather than working together to build a fairer, more just world.

Technological Stagnation and Regression

The rapid pace of technological innovation that defines our current era will grind to a halt in this future of division and conflict. Without the global cooperation necessary to tackle the ethical and logistical challenges of new technologies, breakthroughs in artificial intelligence, biotechnology, and clean energy will slow, and the immense potential of human ingenuity will be wasted. Worse still, the advancements we do make may be weaponized, used by competing nations or corporations to gain an advantage over their rivals rather than to benefit humanity as a whole.

Example: In a world where competition dominates, we may see the rise of dangerous technologies that increase surveillance, restrict personal freedoms, or intensify military conflict. AI, rather than being developed for the collective good, could be used to strengthen authoritarian regimes, monitor citizens, and wage cyberwarfare. Biotechnology, instead of eradicating disease, could be monopolized by a handful of corporations, offering life-saving treatments only to the wealthy. The space race, once a symbol of human ambition, could become another battleground, with nations competing for resources on the moon or Mars rather than collaborating in the pursuit of discovery.

In this future, humanity's potential is wasted, not because we lack the knowledge or capability, but because we are too divided to use it for the common good.
But if we succeed—if we embrace our shared human identity—the future we unlock will be one of peace, innovation, and prosperity that benefits all of

humanity.

A Future of Global Peace

In a world where we embrace global citizenship, where the concept of nationality is replaced by our shared human identity, the idea of war becomes obsolete. Without the artificial divisions of race, religion, and nationality, there is no reason to fight. Instead of nations competing for power and resources, humanity works together to ensure that everyone has access to what they need to survive and thrive. Disputes, when they arise, are resolved through dialogue and cooperation, not violence.

Example: In this future, the trillions of dollars currently spent on military budgets around the world are redirected toward education, healthcare, and infrastructure. Instead of building weapons of war, we build hospitals, schools, and sustainable cities. Former adversaries, once locked in conflict, now work together to promote peace, stability, and the well-being of all people. Nations that were once divided by ethnic or religious strife now collaborate as part of a global community, united by the belief that every human life has value.

Environmental Restoration and Sustainability

The environmental devastation of the past is reversed through collective action and global cooperation. Humanity recognizes that the planet is a shared resource, one that must be protected for future generations. In this future, we have not only halted climate change but have actively restored the damage we caused to the Earth's ecosystems. Clean energy powers the world, forests have been regrown, and the oceans are once again teeming with life.

Example: Renewable energy sources—solar, wind, and geothermal—have replaced fossil fuels entirely. Mega-solar projects in deserts across the world provide clean energy to every continent, while advanced carbon capture technologies reduce greenhouse gases in the atmosphere. Reforestation efforts have restored the Amazon rainforest, while protected marine areas ensure that fish populations and coral reefs thrive. Water, once a scarce resource in many parts of the world, is abundant and accessible to all, thanks to advancements in desalination and sustainable agriculture.

Humanity now lives in harmony with the environment, understanding that the health of the planet is intrinsically linked to our own survival. No longer do we exploit nature for short-term gain; instead, we nurture and protect it, recognizing that a healthy planet means a healthy future for all.

Economic Equality and Shared Prosperity

In a world where we have embraced global citizenship, the economic systems that once perpetuated inequality have been restructured to ensure that wealth and resources are shared more fairly. No longer are a few nations or individuals able to hoard the world's riches at the expense of billions. Instead, global institutions ensure that everyone has access to basic necessities, and the wealth generated by human innovation is distributed equitably.

Example: In this future, poverty has been eradicated. Every person has access to clean water, nutritious food, quality education, and healthcare. No child is born into a life of deprivation. The global economy, once driven by consumption and competition, is now focused on sustainability and fairness. Small businesses and entrepreneurs flourish, with support from global investment funds that prioritize ethical and sustainable practices. Workers, regardless of where they live, are paid fair wages, and the exploitation of labor is a relic of the past.

Innovation and Human Flourishing

With the barriers of nationalism and cultural division dismantled, the full potential of human innovation is unleashed. Scientists, engineers, and thinkers from all over the world collaborate freely, sharing knowledge and resources to solve humanity's greatest challenges. Technological advancements are no longer driven by profit or competition, but by the desire to improve the human condition. Space exploration, medical breakthroughs, and clean energy technologies are developed not for the benefit of a few, but for the betterment of all.

Example: In this future, humanity has achieved monumental feats. Cancer has been cured, thanks to global collaboration in medical research. Energy is free and abundant, provided by limitless renewable sources. The technological gap between developed and developing nations has been closed, as knowledge and resources are shared freely. Space exploration has taken us to Mars and beyond, with humans working together to explore the stars and expand our understanding of the universe.

A Future Where Humanity Flourishes

In this future, humanity not only survives but thrives. With the shackles of cultural division broken, we have unlocked the full potential of cooperation, creativity, and compassion. We no longer view ourselves as divided by nationality, race, or religion. We see ourselves as part of one human family, united in our efforts to build a world where everyone can live with dignity, purpose, and hope.

This is the future we can create if we are willing to embrace our shared human identity. It is a future of peace, environmental restoration, economic equality, and technological progress. A future where humanity reaches its full potential—not because we fought for dominance, but because we chose to work together for the good of all.

Historical Examples of Cultural Conflict

Human history is marked by extraordinary

achievements—scientific discoveries, philosophical advancements, and moments of profound human connection. But alongside these triumphs, our past is also stained by a darker reality: the constant and devastating impact of cultural divisions. Time and time again, humanity has allowed itself to be fractured along the lines of race, religion, ethnicity, and nationality. These artificial boundaries, drawn in the minds of people, have led to conflict, violence, and unimaginable suffering.

From the earliest recorded conflicts to the modern era, cultural divisions have served as catalysts for war, genocide, and systemic oppression. Leaders and governments have exploited these differences to consolidate power, fuel hatred, and justify acts of violence. These divisions have led to the rise of ideologies that seek to dehumanize the "other," creating enemies where none should exist, and legitimizing atrocities that have left lasting scars on the human psyche.

The price we have paid for this separation has been incalculable. Entire civilizations have been brought to their knees, millions of lives lost, and countless futures stolen. Cultural divisions have not only caused immediate destruction but have also perpetuated cycles of violence that pass from one generation to the next. Instead of focusing on our shared needs and aspirations, we have fought each other over imagined differences, robbing humanity of its full potential.

The following historical examples stand as grim reminders of how deeply cultural divisions have harmed us. Each example serves as a testament to the suffering caused when people prioritize cultural identity over their shared humanity. These are not just stories of the past; they are warnings for the future. If we continue to allow cultural divisions to dictate our actions, we risk repeating the same mistakes and perpetuating the cycle of conflict.

These examples illustrate the profound consequences of a world divided by culture—how it has driven people to commit acts of genocide, tear apart nations, and cause suffering on a massive scale. But they also offer lessons that must not be forgotten. If we are to move forward and build a world based on unity and shared identity, we must understand the true cost of division. We must learn from the suffering of the past to create a better future.

1. The Crusades (1095-1291)

The Crusades were a series of religious wars initiated by European Christians in an attempt to reclaim Jerusalem and other holy sites from Muslim control. These wars, fueled by religious and cultural fervor, lasted for nearly 200 years and resulted in the deaths of hundreds of thousands of people. Christians and Muslims, each convinced of the superiority of their own beliefs, fought relentlessly over a piece of land they both deemed sacred.

Reflection: The Crusades remind us of the destruction that occurs when we define ourselves by our religious identities. If Christians and Muslims had recognized their shared humanity, they could have coexisted peacefully instead of spilling blood over religious differences.

2. The Thirty Years' War (1618-1648)

The Thirty Years' War was one of the longest and most brutal conflicts in European history, fought primarily between Catholics and Protestants. Though rooted in religious differences, the war also became a battleground for political power and control over territories. This war devastated Europe, causing millions of deaths, widespread famine, and economic ruin.

Reflection: The Thirty Years' War highlights how religious identity can be weaponized for political gain. If the people and leaders of Europe had recognized their shared interests as human beings rather than dividing along religious lines, they could have spared generations from immense suffering.

3. The Israeli-Palestinian Conflict (1948–Present)

The Israeli-Palestinian conflict is one of the most enduring conflicts in modern history, driven by competing national and religious identities. Both Israelis and Palestinians lay claim to the same land, and the conflict has led to numerous wars, uprisings, and ongoing violence. The situation remains unresolved, with countless lives lost and millions displaced.

Reflection: This conflict illustrates how nationalism and religious identity continue to fuel division. If Israelis and Palestinians embraced a shared human identity, they could begin to move past the cycle of violence and work together to create a state where all people, regardless of their background, live in peace and prosperity.

4. The Rwandan Genocide (1994)

In one of the most horrific genocides of the 20th century, the ethnic divisions between the Hutu and Tutsi populations of Rwanda led to the mass killing of approximately 800,000 people in just 100 days. What began as long-standing ethnic tension escalated into unimaginable violence as Hutus sought to exterminate the Tutsi minority.

Reflection: The Rwandan Genocide shows the deadly consequences of ethnic identity being prioritized over our shared humanity. If Rwandans had rejected the false notion of ethnic superiority and embraced their common human identity, the genocide could have been averted.

5. The Yugoslav Wars (1991-2001)

The breakup of Yugoslavia in the early 1990s was marked by a series of brutal wars, driven largely by ethnic nationalism and cultural divisions. Serbs, Croats, and Bosniaks—who had coexisted for years—

suddenly found themselves divided along ethnic and religious lines, resulting in widespread violence and atrocities.

Reflection: The Yugoslav Wars demonstrate how quickly cultural identity can be exploited to fuel hatred and violence. If the people of the former Yugoslavia had prioritized their shared human identity over their ethnic differences, they might have avoided the bloodshed that tore their countries apart.

6. India-Pakistan Partition and Wars (1947–Present)

When British India was partitioned into two states—India and Pakistan—in 1947, the division was made along religious lines, with India becoming a predominantly Hindu state and Pakistan predominantly Muslim. This partition led to mass migrations, violence, and ongoing tensions between the two countries, resulting in several wars and a nuclear arms race.

Reflection: The partition of India and Pakistan is a clear example of how religious identity can lead to division and conflict. If Hindus and Muslims had embraced their shared human identity, they might have avoided the violence and instability that has plagued the region for decades.

Letting Go of Cultural Identity and Embracing Human Identity

Letting go of cultural identity is not a simple or easy

task. For many, cultural identity forms the core of who they are. It connects them to their history, their ancestors, and the traditions passed down through generations. It is the lens through which they view the world, the stories they tell themselves about their place within it, and the values that guide their decisions. To relinquish such an identity can feel like a deep personal loss—a rejection of everything that shaped them and everything they hold dear. It can feel like a betrayal not only of oneself but of one's family, ancestors, and community.

For those who have been raised to honor their cultural heritage, the idea of moving beyond it can be daunting. It can stir feelings of guilt and disloyalty. After all, cultural identity is often intertwined with a sense of belonging and pride. It represents the struggles and triumphs of one's ancestors, the customs and traditions that have provided meaning and structure for generations. To walk away from that can feel as if one is severing ties with a rich and cherished past.

However, we must confront a difficult truth: while cultural identities may offer comfort and a sense of belonging, they are also a source of division and conflict. These identities, which were meant to bind people together within specific communities, have all too often served to divide humanity as a whole. Cultural identities, when held onto too tightly, become walls that separate people, creating an "us versus them" mentality that fosters distrust, fear, and hostility toward those who are different.

Throughout history, cultural identities have been weaponized by those in power to justify discrimination, oppression, and even genocide. Leaders have used the concept of cultural superiority to rally their followers and wage wars, painting others as enemies simply because they belong to a different group. The deep-seated attachment to cultural identity has led to countless conflicts, both large and small, as people cling to the belief that their race, religion, or ethnicity makes them somehow superior or more deserving of resources, land, or power.

What we must recognize is that cultural identities —while offering a sense of tradition and continuity —are ultimately harmful baggage that holds humanity back. In a world facing unprecedented global challenges, the divisions created by cultural identities prevent us from uniting to solve the problems that affect us all. Climate change, pandemics, economic inequality, and technological disruption do not recognize borders or cultural differences. These are issues that demand collective action and a shared sense of responsibility, yet cultural divisions continue to create barriers to the cooperation we so desperately need.

Clinging to cultural identity keeps us locked in

an outdated way of thinking, one that prioritizes the past over the future. It keeps us focused on what separates us rather than what unites us. By holding onto cultural identity, we carry with us the weight of historical grievances, inherited prejudices, and outdated values that no longer serve the needs of a globalized world. It prevents us from seeing each other as fellow human beings, bound by the same fundamental desires for peace, security, and prosperity.

Moreover, cultural identity can limit personal growth. When we define ourselves solely by the culture we were born into, we restrict our ability to connect with others on a deeper, more meaningful level. We become trapped within the boundaries of that identity, unable to fully explore the richness of the human experience beyond our own cultural framework. This isolation stifles empathy, creativity, and understanding, perpetuating the very divisions that have caused so much harm throughout history.

To move forward, we must be willing to let go of the cultural baggage that holds us back. This does not mean forgetting our history or dishonoring our ancestors, but rather recognizing that the world we live in today demands a new way of thinking —one that embraces our shared human identity over the narrow confines of cultural heritage. We must acknowledge that while cultural traditions can offer insight into the past, they are not the path forward. The future requires us to think beyond the limitations of race, religion, or ethnicity and to see ourselves as part of a larger, interconnected human family.

Letting go of cultural identity may feel like a loss at first, but it is ultimately an opportunity for liberation. It frees us from the constraints of the past and allows us to build a future that is not defined by the divisions that once separated us. By embracing a human identity—one that transcends the superficial differences of culture—we can unlock the potential for true unity, collaboration, and progress. We can begin to address the global challenges that threaten our survival, not as members of competing cultural groups, but as human beings working together for the common good.

In the end, letting go of cultural identity is not about rejecting our past; it is about choosing our future. It is about recognizing that the survival and flourishing of humanity depend on our ability to transcend the divisions that have caused so much suffering and to embrace a new identity—one that is inclusive, forward-thinking, and focused on the well-being of all people, regardless of their background.

The world is changing, and the challenges we face are too great to be solved by isolated communities or divided nations. Now, more than ever, we need to see ourselves as part of a global community, united by a shared purpose and a common identity. By letting go of cultural identity, we free ourselves to create a world where cooperation, empathy, and mutual respect are the driving forces behind our actions—a world where humanity can truly flourish.

1. The Emotional Challenge of Letting Go

Cultural identity is deeply ingrained in the human experience. It is more than just a set of traditions, customs, or beliefs—it is a connection to something larger than oneself, a link to one's ancestors, heritage, and the community that shaped one's worldview. Cultural identity provides a sense of belonging, a narrative of where we come from and who we are. It often defines our values, our way of life, and how we relate to others. Letting go of this identity can feel like severing ties with the very essence of one's history and upbringing. It can feel like an abandonment of the struggles and sacrifices made by previous generations to preserve that culture. This sense of betrayal—of losing the stories, lessons, and wisdom passed down through generations—creates a profound emotional struggle.

For many, cultural identity is a source of pride. It is through cultural traditions that we celebrate life's milestones, express our beliefs, and connect with others who share the same heritage. It is where we find comfort in times of hardship and community in times of celebration. To let go of this is not merely a rational decision; it is an emotional upheaval that strikes at the core of what makes us feel connected to our past. It may feel as though we are turning our back on the struggles of our ancestors, those who fought to preserve their culture against forces of oppression, assimilation, or erasure.

The weight of this emotional attachment cannot be understated. People often fear that by letting go of their cultural identity, they will lose a part of themselves—an integral piece of their identity that has shaped their beliefs, values, and even their sense of morality. This fear is compounded by the idea that abandoning cultural traditions and norms is a betrayal of the community that nurtured and supported them. In societies where cultural identity is tied to religious, ethnic, or national pride, this feeling of betrayal can be even more intense, as it is not just a personal loss but a perceived collective one.

The emotional struggle is further complicated by the fact that cultural identity is often intertwined with a sense of duty or loyalty. We are taught from a young age to honor the past, to carry forward the traditions of our ancestors, and to take pride in the culture we inherit. This inheritance is not just a passive part of our identity; it is actively cultivated and reinforced through rituals, language, customs, and shared experiences. The thought of letting go of these practices can provoke guilt and internal conflict, as though we are erasing the memories of those who came before us. The emotional pain of distancing oneself from this deeply embedded identity can be sharp, as it can feel like turning away from the very foundation upon which one's life has been built.

However, while the emotional struggle of letting go of cultural identity is very real, it is crucial to understand that clinging to the past in this way can perpetuate division, conflict, and suffering. The same cultural identities that give us a sense of belonging and pride are often the very forces that divide us from others. Throughout history, these identities have been used as tools of exclusion, defining who is "in" and who is "out," who belongs and who is an outsider. This process of othering creates barriers between people, fostering fear, suspicion, and hostility toward those who do not share the same identity.

When we cling too tightly to cultural identity, we risk reinforcing the divisions that have fueled countless conflicts. From religious wars to ethnic cleansings, from the persecution of minority groups to the rise of nationalism, cultural identities have often been wielded as weapons to justify oppression, hatred, and violence. People who define themselves solely through the lens of their cultural identity may become blind to the humanity of others, viewing those who are different as threats to their way of life. This insularity breeds conflict, as people feel compelled to protect their identity at all costs, even if it means perpetuating cycles of violence and division.

In clinging to cultural identity, we also limit our ability to grow as individuals and as a society. Cultural identity can act as a lens through which we view the world, but it can also become a set of blinders, narrowing our perspective and preventing us from seeing the common humanity that exists beyond the boundaries of race, religion, or nationality. When we define ourselves primarily by our cultural heritage, we may fail to recognize the shared values, aspirations, and struggles that unite us with people from different backgrounds. This prevents us from reaching out, forming meaningful connections, and working together to solve the global challenges we all face.

Moreover, by holding onto cultural identities, we perpetuate the historical grievances that have divided humanity for centuries. The conflicts between cultures are often rooted in past wrongs— wars, invasions, colonization, religious persecution —that have left deep scars. While these historical events must be remembered and understood, clinging to them as part of our identity keeps us tethered to the pain, anger, and resentment of the past. It becomes difficult to move forward when we are constantly looking backward, reliving the conflicts of our ancestors and allowing those conflicts to shape our present actions.

Letting go of cultural identity does not mean erasing history or denying the importance of tradition. It means recognizing that the future cannot be built on the divisions of the past. It means understanding that while cultural identities may have served a purpose in times when humanity was more fragmented, they are no longer adequate in an interconnected, globalized world. The challenges we face—climate change, economic inequality, pandemics—demand that we transcend the boundaries of culture and embrace a shared human identity.

This does not mean we must forget the lessons of our ancestors or abandon the wisdom they passed down. Rather, it means choosing to prioritize the values that unite us as human beings over the identities that divide us. It means recognizing that clinging to cultural identity out of fear of loss will only lead to more suffering, more conflict, and more division. It is by embracing our common humanity, rather than our cultural differences, that we can begin to heal the wounds of the past and build a future that benefits all.

Letting go of cultural identity is not about rejecting one's roots—it is about freeing oneself from the constraints of division and stepping into a world where cooperation, empathy, and shared purpose define our interactions. It is about realizing that the things that truly matter—compassion, justice, equality—are not tied to any one culture but are universal values that transcend all borders. By embracing these values and moving beyond the limitations of cultural identity, we can unlock the potential for global peace, innovation, and progress. In doing so, we not only honor the best of our past but also create the opportunity for a better, more unified future.

2. Why We Must Abandon Cultural Identity

Cultural identities have historically created boundaries between people, reinforcing divisions that prevent us from recognizing our common humanity. Over time, these boundaries—based on race, religion, and nationality—have been deeply ingrained in the way society's function. While cultural identities may offer a sense of belonging and familiarity, they have also served as powerful tools of separation. Instead of bringing people together, these identities have been wielded to divide humanity, to emphasize difference rather than unity.

Race, for example, has long been used to categorize and differentiate people based on superficial characteristics like skin color, often leading to the false belief that certain races are inherently superior or inferior. This belief has fueled systems of oppression, such as slavery, colonialism, apartheid, and racial segregation. For centuries, racial identities have been manipulated by those in power to justify discrimination and inequality, creating a legacy of injustice that continues to affect people to this day. The very idea of race—something that has no biological basis—has been used to construct walls between people, fostering fear, hatred, and division where none should exist.

Similarly, religion, which at its core seeks to provide meaning, connection, and a sense of purpose, has often been exploited to create division. Religious identities have been weaponized by leaders to incite violence, as seen in the Crusades, the Thirty Years' War, or the numerous conflicts between Hindus and Muslims on the Indian subcontinent. Instead of fostering empathy and understanding, religious identity has frequently been used to define who belongs and who does not, marking those outside the faith as enemies, heretics, or infidels. The cultural baggage tied to religious identity has led to persecution, religious wars, and the suppression of freedom of thought, all of which hinder humanity's ability to coexist peacefully.

Nationality, too, has been a source of division. Nationalism, the belief that one's country is superior to others, has fuelled centuries of conflict—from the rise of imperialism to the two World Wars of the 20th century. The idea that people from different nations are fundamentally opposed has been used to justify militarization, expansionism, and colonialism. National borders, which are little more than arbitrary lines drawn on a map, have been treated as sacrosanct, and people have been taught to prioritize their national identity over their identity as human beings. This has led to xenophobia, isolationism, and policies that prioritize national interests at the expense of global cooperation.

While these identities—racial, religious, and national—can offer comfort by providing a sense of belonging and continuity, they have also trapped us in cycles of prejudice, rivalry, and exclusion. They provide a familiar narrative, but that narrative often tells us that our group, our race, our religion, or our nation is somehow better or more important than others. This mindset prevents us from embracing our shared humanity and recognizing the fundamental truth that we are all members of the same species, with the same basic needs and aspirations.

The danger of clinging to cultural identities is that we carry with us the conflicts and prejudices of the past. We inherit the biases, divisions, and hatreds that have shaped human history. When we define ourselves by these narrow identities, we are bound to repeat the mistakes of those who came before us. The wars, genocides, and injustices that have marred human history were often driven by a belief in the supremacy of one cultural group over another. By holding on to these identities, we perpetuate the myth that our differences are more important than what we share in common.

Cultural identity, in its most rigid form, binds us to outdated values and systems that are no longer useful for the survival of our species. Many of the traditions, customs, and beliefs that have been passed down through generations were shaped by the specific circumstances of the past. They were often developed in response to threats—real or perceived—from outside groups. These values may have served a purpose in a more isolated, fragmented world, but in an age of global interconnection, they become barriers to progress. What once might have been protective—such as tribalism or suspicion of outsiders—now prevents us from addressing the shared challenges we face as a species.

For example, nationalism may have served to unify a country in times of war or conflict, but in today's world, it creates division and isolation at a time when international cooperation is critical for solving global problems like climate change, pandemics, and economic inequality. Religious dogma, which might have provided social cohesion in centuries past, can now hinder scientific advancement, stifle critical thinking, and prevent people from embracing progressive ideas that promote equality and human rights. Racial identities, which were historically used to justify systems of hierarchy and control, continue to perpetuate inequality, preventing societies from becoming truly inclusive.

By holding on to these cultural identities, we are weighed down by the cultural baggage of the past—baggage that includes division, rivalry, and exclusion. This baggage prevents humanity from progressing into a future where cooperation, empathy, and shared purpose are the guiding principles of our actions. It keeps us locked in a zero-sum game, where one group's success is seen as a threat to another's, and where differences are viewed with suspicion rather than curiosity and respect.

The cultural baggage we carry also limits our capacity for innovation and global problem-solving. In a world where cultural divisions dominate, collaboration across borders becomes more difficult. People are less likely to work together when they are entrenched in a mindset of competition and distrust. This prevents the free flow of ideas, resources, and talent that is necessary for addressing the world's most pressing issues. When we cling to cultural identities, we close ourselves off from the possibility of collective progress, focusing instead on protecting our own group's interests at the expense of the global good.

Ultimately, cultural identity, when used as a tool for division, stunts humanity's growth. It prevents us from seeing the world through a lens of shared responsibility, mutual respect, and collaboration. It keeps us bound to the conflicts of the past, unable to imagine a future where humanity is united by common goals and shared values. If we are to survive the challenges that lie ahead—environmental degradation, resource scarcity, political instability—we must be willing to let go of the cultural baggage that has weighed us down for so long.

The path forward requires us to embrace our shared humanity and to recognize that the divisions we have clung to are no longer relevant. The future demands a new way of thinking, one that prioritizes unity over separation, cooperation over conflict, and human identity over cultural differences. Only by shedding the cultural identities that have divided us can we truly progress as a species and build a world where everyone has the opportunity to thrive.

3. The Rewards of Human Identity

By discarding the cultural baggage that has weighed us down for centuries, we open the door to a transformative fresh start—one that is not bound by the limitations of the past or constrained by the divisions that have long defined human relationships. This fresh start offers humanity the chance to redefine itself, not based on historical grievances, inherited prejudices, or the artificial boundaries of race, religion, or nationality, but on the potential of what we can achieve together. By embracing a human identity, we shift our focus from the conflicts and divisions that have held us back, allowing us to build a future based on cooperation, empathy, and shared progress.

The cultural baggage that we carry is heavy, accumulated over centuries of conflict, division, and mistrust. It is the product of a world where people were taught to fear those who are different, to compete for resources, and to protect their own cultural group at the expense of others. This baggage includes the weight of historical grievances—wars fought over territory, religion, or race; colonization and its aftermath; systemic racism, apartheid, and other forms of oppression. These legacies of division continue to shape the way we see the world today, influencing how we relate to others, how we view conflict, and how we understand our place in the world.

Yet, as we carry this cultural baggage, we are also weighed down by inherited prejudices—biases and assumptions passed down from generation to generation. These prejudices may be subtle or overt, but they have been ingrained in the fabric of societies for centuries. Whether it's the belief in racial superiority, religious exclusivity, or national exceptionalism, these prejudices have created invisible walls between people, walls that prevent us from seeing each other as fellow human beings with the same fundamental needs, desires, and dreams. These inherited beliefs keep us locked in patterns of rivalry and exclusion, making it difficult to work together toward common goals.

When we hold onto cultural baggage, we allow the wounds of the past to continue festering. The conflicts and grievances of our ancestors—though they may no longer be relevant to the modern world—continue to shape our interactions with others. Old animosities linger, passed down like family heirlooms, even when the original causes of those conflicts have long since faded. The bitterness, mistrust, and hostility that come with these inherited conflicts prevent us from fully embracing the possibility of a peaceful and cooperative future. We remain trapped in cycles of retribution, unable to move forward because we are too focused on settling old scores or preserving a cultural identity that, in many cases, no longer serves us.

However, when we choose to discard this cultural baggage, we free ourselves from these constraints. We allow ourselves the opportunity for a fresh start—one in which our relationships with others are not defined by the divisions of the past, but by the potential for collaboration and mutual respect. Letting go of cultural identity does not mean forgetting our history or ignoring the lessons of the past; it means recognizing that the future cannot be built on old grievances and that our survival as a species depends on our ability to unite rather than divide.

This fresh start is about embracing a new

identity, one that is rooted not in the narrow confines of cultural heritage, but in our shared human experience. A human identity transcends the boundaries of race, religion, and nationality. It acknowledges that, while we may come from different backgrounds and have different experiences, we are all part of the same species. We share the same planet, the same resources, and the same future. By identifying as part of the human race, we shift our perspective from what separates us to what unites us.

A human identity allows us to focus on what we can achieve together moving forward, rather than where we have been divided in the past. It encourages us to look beyond the tribal instincts that have shaped human history, to move away from the mindset of "us versus them" and to embrace a new way of thinking—one that prioritizes cooperation, empathy, and shared responsibility. When we see ourselves as members of the same global community, the need for conflict diminishes. We are no longer in competition with one another for dominance or resources; instead, we are collaborators, working together to solve the challenges that affect us all.

The potential for true global unity is unlocked when we let go of cultural divisions and embrace our shared human identity. Global unity does not mean uniformity—it does not require us to erase the rich diversity of human expression, but rather to celebrate that diversity in a way that fosters inclusion, cooperation, and respect. When we identify as part of the human race, we create the conditions for a world where people from all walks of life can contribute their talents, skills, and knowledge to the collective good. No longer constrained by the divisions of race or nationality, people are free to collaborate across borders, sharing ideas, resources, and solutions to the global challenges we face.

In a world defined by human identity, cooperation becomes the driving force behind progress. Instead of nations or cultural groups competing for limited resources or jockeying for power, the focus shifts to how we can work together to ensure that everyone has access to what they need. Whether it's addressing climate change, developing new technologies, or creating systems for equitable distribution of resources, cooperation allows us to pool our strengths and knowledge to find solutions that benefit all of humanity. Cooperation, driven by a sense of shared responsibility, enables us to tackle problems that no single nation or group could solve on its own.

Cooperation also fosters innovation. When people from diverse backgrounds come together to work on a common goal, they bring with them a wealth of perspectives and ideas. By removing the barriers that cultural divisions create, we open the door to new ways of thinking and problem-solving. Collaboration across borders and cultures can lead to breakthroughs in science, technology, and medicine that would have been impossible in a world constrained by competition and mistrust. The combined efforts of the brightest minds from around the world can accelerate progress in ways that benefit all of humanity, rather than just a select few.

At the heart of a human identity is empathy—the ability to understand and share the feelings of others. Empathy is what allows us to connect with people beyond our immediate cultural group and to see their struggles and joys as our own. When we embrace a human identity, we cultivate a sense of empathy that transcends cultural boundaries. We begin to see all people, regardless of their race, religion, or nationality, as deserving of dignity, respect, and compassion. Empathy drives us to act not just in our own interest, but in the interest of others. It encourages us to build systems that support the well-being of all people, rather than just those who belong to our cultural group.

Empathy also replaces the fear and suspicion that often arise from cultural differences. When we identify as part of the human race, we no longer see others as threats simply because they are different. Instead, we recognize our common humanity and approach interactions with an open mind and heart. This shift in perspective reduces the likelihood of conflict, as people are more likely to engage in dialogue, understanding, and cooperation when they see each other as equals. Empathy, coupled with cooperation, creates the foundation for a world where conflict is no longer driven by cultural division, but is resolved through collaboration and mutual respect.

The potential for peace is greatly enhanced in a world where human identity prevails over cultural identity. The divisions that have historically fueled wars, genocide, and oppression are rendered irrelevant in the face of a shared human identity. People are no longer motivated to fight over differences that, in the grand scheme of things, are superficial. Instead, the focus is on how we can live together harmoniously, respecting each other's rights and working together to create a more just and equitable world. The absence of cultural division reduces the incentives for violence and conflict, as people no longer see themselves as separate from or superior to others.

The shift from cultural identity to human identity also allows us to address the root causes of global challenges. Environmental degradation, poverty, inequality, and political instability are all issues that require a collective response. By embracing a human identity, we move beyond the parochial concerns of individual nations or cultural groups and recognize that the well-being of humanity as a whole is at stake. This perspective encourages us to take action on a global scale, whether it's reducing carbon emissions, addressing the refugee crisis, or creating policies that promote social and economic justice.

Ultimately, identifying as part of the human race creates the potential for a world united by shared values, goals, and a commitment to the common good. It allows us to build a future that is not defined by the limitations of the past, but by the possibilities of what we can achieve together. By discarding the cultural baggage of division, rivalry, and exclusion, we free ourselves to create a world where cooperation, empathy, and peace are the guiding principles of human interaction.

This is the power of embracing a human identity—it is the key to unlocking humanity's full potential. It is the foundation upon which we can build a future where all people, regardless of their background, have the opportunity to thrive. It is a future where we are no longer held back by the divisions of the past, but where we are united by a shared vision of progress, justice, and peace.

Comparing the European Union and African Union: A Study in Borders and Identity

Both the European Union (EU) and the African Union (AU) offer valuable lessons on the potential benefits of removing borders, but they also highlight the limitations of integration when cultural identity remains intact.

1. The European Union: A Model of Economic Success with Lingering Divisions

The European Union has successfully promoted economic and political cooperation by removing internal borders, allowing for the free movement of people, goods, and services. However, the EU continues to grapple with divisions rooted in national and cultural identity. Nationalism is on the rise in several EU member states, and events like Brexit demonstrate how cultural divisions still influence political decisions.

Example: The EU's response to the 2008 global financial crisis demonstrates the benefits of regional cooperation. Through collective action, the EU managed to stabilize the eurozone and help member states recover. However, nationalism still threatens the union's cohesion, as seen in the rise of far-right movements in countries like Hungary and Poland, which resist EU-wide policies on immigration and multiculturalism.

2. The African Union: Aspirations of Unity Amidst Deep Divisions

The African Union seeks to promote political integration and economic development across Africa. However, the deep-rooted ethnic and cultural diversity of the continent has made this vision difficult to achieve. Internal conflicts, driven by ethnic and national divisions, have hampered efforts toward unity.

Example: The African Continental Free Trade Area (AfCFTA) is one of the AU's most ambitious initiatives, seeking to create a single market across Africa. However, the progress of AfCFTA has been slowed by political instability, weak infrastructure, and internal ethnic conflicts, demonstrating how cultural divisions can hinder regional integration.

3. What Could Be Achieved Without Cultural and Ethnic Divisions?

Both the EU and the AU offer valuable lessons: while removing borders brings undeniable benefits, it is not enough to overcome the deep-rooted divisions caused by cultural and ethnic identity. If the people of Europe and Africa fully embraced a human identity, the potential for cooperation would be limitless, and both regions could achieve even greater prosperity and unity.

Becoming a Global Citizen: The Path Forward
1. What it Means to Be a Global Citizen

Global citizenship is not merely a political or economic stance; it is a radical and transformative shift in how we view ourselves, the world, and our place within it. At its core, global citizenship represents a complete reimagining of identity—one that transcends the limitations of nationality, race, religion, and culture to embrace a more expansive and inclusive understanding of what it means to be human. A global citizen is someone who sees the world not as a collection of separate and isolated nations, but as a single, interconnected community, where the well-being of every individual is bound to the well-being of all.

This shift in perspective requires a fundamental re-evaluation of the systems and structures that have shaped human society for centuries. Historically, people have defined themselves by the nation they were born in, the religion they were raised in, or the ethnic group they belong to. These identities provided a sense of belonging and security in a world that often felt uncertain or dangerous. But as the world has become increasingly interconnected through globalization, technology, and communication, the limitations of these narrow identities have become glaringly apparent. Global citizenship challenges the notion that our primary loyalty should be to our nation, religion, or culture. Instead, it asks us to expand our sense of belonging to include all of humanity, recognizing that the divisions that once seemed so significant are, in reality, artificial and increasingly irrelevant.

To be a global citizen is to recognize that the challenges we face—climate change, pandemics, inequality, and conflict—cannot be solved by any one country acting alone. These are global problems that require global solutions, and those solutions can only be achieved through cooperation and collaboration on a scale that transcends national borders. The future of humanity depends on our ability to work together, as one global community, to address these challenges. Global citizenship is, therefore, not just a matter of ideology or philosophy; it is a survival imperative. The interconnected nature of our world means that what happens in one part of the planet can have profound and far-reaching effects on the rest of it. A global citizen understands that their actions—whether they are related to environmental sustainability, economic justice, or human rights—have consequences that extend far beyond their immediate surroundings.

One of the most significant aspects of global citizenship is its rejection of the "us versus them" mentality that has long dominated human history. Traditionally, people have been taught to view those outside their nation, religion, or culture as "others"—people who are fundamentally different, and often inferior. This mindset has fueled countless conflicts, from wars and colonization to genocide and systemic discrimination. Global citizenship, by contrast, promotes a sense of shared identity and mutual responsibility. It asks us to see people from different countries and cultures not as strangers or threats, but as fellow human beings with whom we share the same basic needs and aspirations. A global citizen recognizes that the differences between people—whether they are cultural, linguistic, or religious—are far less important than the common humanity that unites us all.

This shift in perspective has profound implications for how we approach issues of justice, equality, and human rights. A global citizen does not limit their concern to the well-being of their fellow citizens; instead, they feel a sense of responsibility for the well-being of all people, regardless of where they live or what cultural group they belong to. This means that a global citizen advocates for human rights not just within their own borders, but for people everywhere. They understand that injustice anywhere is a threat to justice everywhere, and that the suffering of others diminishes the humanity of us all. In a world where millions of people are still denied their basic human rights—whether it is access to clean water, education, or freedom from violence—a global citizen recognizes that these issues cannot be ignored simply because they occur in another country.

A key component of global citizenship is empathy —the ability to understand and share the feelings of others, even when their experiences may seem far removed from our own. Empathy allows global citizens to transcend the limitations of their own experiences and to connect with people who may live in different circumstances or come from different backgrounds. It is this sense of empathy that drives global citizens to take action on behalf of others, whether it is by supporting international development projects, advocating for refugee rights, or participating in movements to address climate change. Empathy enables global citizens to see the world through the eyes of others and to recognize that the struggles faced by people in distant places are not so different from their own.

Global citizenship also involves a deep commitment to sustainability and the recognition that the Earth's resources are finite and must be used responsibly. A global citizen understands that environmental degradation, pollution, and climate change are not isolated problems that can be dealt with by individual nations. These are global challenges that require collective action. The choices we make about energy consumption, food production, and waste management have consequences not only for the environment but for people around the world —especially those in vulnerable and marginalized communities who are often the most affected by climate change and environmental disasters. A global citizen feels a responsibility to future generations and is committed to living in a way that ensures the health and sustainability of the planet for all people.

Economically, global citizenship calls for a more equitable and just distribution of resources. The current global economic system is deeply unequal, with a small percentage of the world's population controlling the majority of its wealth, while billions of people live in poverty. A global citizen recognizes that this inequality is not just a moral failing, but a systemic problem that requires global solutions. Global citizenship promotes economic justice by advocating for fair trade, workers' rights, and the redistribution of resources to ensure that everyone has access to basic necessities like food, clean water, healthcare, and education. It challenges the idea that wealth and resources should be concentrated in the hands of a few, and instead promotes a vision of a world where prosperity is shared and everyone has the opportunity to thrive.

In the realm of governance, global citizenship challenges the traditional model of the nation-state as the primary unit of political organization. While global citizens respect the sovereignty of nations, they also recognize that the most pressing issues facing humanity—such as climate change, pandemics, and global inequality—cannot be solved within the confines of national borders. As such, global citizens advocate for stronger international institutions and global governance structures that can effectively address these transnational challenges. This does not mean the dissolution of national governments, but rather the creation of global frameworks that allow for cooperation and collective action on a scale that matches the complexity of the problems we face. Global citizens support initiatives like the United Nations, the World Health Organization, and international treaties such as the Paris Agreement on climate change, recognizing that these institutions, while imperfect, are essential for fostering global cooperation.

Education is another critical component of global citizenship. A global citizen understands that education is not just about acquiring knowledge or skills for personal advancement; it is about becoming informed and engaged members of the global community. Global citizenship education encourages people to think critically about the world around them, to question systems of inequality and injustice, and to seek out opportunities for collaboration and positive change. It fosters an understanding of global interdependence and the ways in which our actions—whether as individuals or as members of larger communities—affect people and ecosystems far beyond our immediate environment. By promoting a sense of global responsibility, education empowers people to act on issues that matter, whether through advocacy, volunteerism, or careers dedicated to social and environmental justice.

At its heart, global citizenship is about embracing a new vision of identity—one that is not bound by the arbitrary divisions of race, religion, or nationality. It is a recognition that the most important identity we hold is not that of a citizen of any one country, but of a citizen of the world. This does not mean that we must abandon our cultural heritage or national pride; rather, it means that we must expand our sense of identity to include the whole of humanity. Global citizenship asks us to recognize that our fates are intertwined, that our well-being is connected to the well-being of others, and that the challenges we face can only be overcome if we work together.

In embracing global citizenship, we commit ourselves to a set of values that prioritize cooperation, empathy, and justice. We reject the notion that our differences should divide us, and instead, we celebrate the diversity that makes humanity so rich and dynamic. We understand that the world's problems are too big to be solved by any one country or group, and that the solutions require collective effort, shared responsibility, and a commitment to the common good. Global citizenship is not just about changing the way we think; it is about changing the way we act, both in our personal lives and in the global arena.

A global citizen is someone who sees the world not through the narrow lens of nationalism or cultural superiority, but through the broader lens of shared humanity. They understand that borders are not the defining features of our world, but rather temporary lines that can and should be transcended. They see themselves not as isolated individuals, but as part of a global community, united by common values and common challenges. And they recognize that the future of humanity depends on our ability to embrace this new way of thinking, to work together, and to build a world where everyone, regardless of where they come from, can live with dignity, justice, and hope.

2. How Grassroots Movements Can Drive Change

Grassroots movements must lead the charge in promoting the ideals of global citizenship. While top-down political change is often slow and constrained by existing power structures, it is the energy and passion of grassroots activism that has the power to spark widespread transformation. These movements —born out of local communities but capable of expanding to a global scale—are uniquely positioned to challenge the status quo, demand accountability, and inspire a shift in how people see themselves, their communities, and the world. By organizing at both the local and global levels, grassroots movements can mobilize ordinary citizens to push for leaders who prioritize global cooperation and human identity over nationalism, cultural divisions, and narrow political interests.

In an era where traditional political systems often seem unresponsive or entrenched in outdated ideas, grassroots movements offer a powerful means for people to take control of their future. Global citizenship—the belief that one's primary allegiance should be to humanity as a whole rather than to a specific nation, culture, or religion—must become the rallying cry of these movements. By advocating for policies that prioritize the well-being of all people, regardless of where they live or what cultural group they belong to, grassroots activists can challenge the divisive ideologies that have kept humanity fragmented and unable to address the global challenges that threaten our collective survival.

One of the most significant advantages of grassroots movements is their ability to transcend national borders. Unlike traditional political systems, which are often confined by geographical boundaries, grassroots movements are fluid, dynamic, and capable of spanning continents. They have the power to connect people from different backgrounds and regions around shared concerns, creating a sense of solidarity that is not limited by nationality or culture. These movements can galvanize people to see themselves not just as citizens of their local communities or countries, but as part of a larger human family. This shift in perspective is essential for fostering the sense of shared responsibility that lies at the heart of global citizenship.

Local organization is the foundation of any grassroots movement, but in the digital age, local efforts can quickly grow into global phenomena. Social media, online platforms, and other digital tools allow grassroots activists to amplify their voices and connect with like-minded individuals around the world. A protest in one city can spark a wave of demonstrations across the globe, as people realize that the issues they face—whether related to climate change, inequality, or human rights—are not isolated problems but part of a larger, interconnected struggle. These movements can spread rapidly, transcending cultural and geographical barriers as people recognize that the solutions to global problems require collective action.

Grassroots movements have historically played a crucial role in challenging entrenched systems of power and bringing about significant social and political change. The Civil Rights Movement in the United States, the anti-apartheid movement in South Africa, and the feminist movements around the world are just a few examples of how grassroots activism has transformed societies. These movements did not wait for change to come from above; they demanded it from below, using their collective power to force leaders to listen, to act, and to reform. In the same way, the promotion of global citizenship will require grassroots movements to rise up and demand that political leaders prioritize global cooperation, equity, and sustainability over narrow national interests.

One powerful example of how grassroots movements can promote global citizenship is the Fridays for Future movement, led by climate activist Greta Thunberg. What began as a single teenager protesting outside the Swedish parliament has grown into a global movement involving millions of people across more than 150 countries. This movement demonstrates how grassroots activism can transcend national borders and inspire people from diverse backgrounds to come together around shared concerns. Fridays for Future is not bound by any one nationality or cultural identity; it is a movement driven by the recognition that climate change is a global problem that requires global solutions. The movement's success lies in its ability to mobilize ordinary people—students, parents, workers, and activists—into a collective force that demands change.

Fridays for Future is a perfect example of how grassroots movements can embody the principles of global citizenship. It has shown that people, regardless of where they live, care about the same fundamental issues—clean air, water, and a livable planet for future generations. It has encouraged people to see themselves as part of a global community with a shared responsibility to protect the Earth and its inhabitants. By focusing on a cause that transcends national borders, Fridays for Future has highlighted the limitations of nationalist and isolationist policies that prioritize short-term economic gain over the long-term health of the planet. The movement has also demonstrated that young people, in particular, are ready to challenge the political and economic systems that have perpetuated environmental destruction and inequality.

But the impact of grassroots movements goes beyond the environmental sphere. These movements have the potential to reshape global politics by pushing for leaders who embrace global citizenship as a guiding principle. As grassroots activists organize and demand change, they can influence elections, campaigns, and policies. By mobilizing voters to support candidates who prioritize international cooperation, climate action, human rights, and social justice, grassroots movements can help elect leaders who are committed to building a world where humanity thrives as a united, interdependent community. This influence can be seen in movements advocating for human rights, gender equality, and economic justice, where grassroots activism has played a pivotal role in holding governments accountable and demanding reforms.

The influence of grassroots movements also lies in their ability to educate and raise awareness. By organizing protests, campaigns, workshops, and public forums, these movements can expose the public to the realities of global challenges that might otherwise be ignored. Through this process of education and engagement, grassroots activists can help people understand that the problems facing their local communities—whether economic inequality, environmental degradation, or social injustice—are part of a broader global crisis. They can encourage people to think beyond the narrow confines of their immediate environment and to recognize that their fate is tied to the fate of others around the world. This awareness is critical in fostering the empathy and solidarity that are essential for global citizenship.

Moreover, grassroots movements have the power to create lasting cultural change. They challenge the assumptions and values that have long underpinned nationalist and isolationist ideologies. By advocating for global citizenship, these movements can help shift public perception away from divisive concepts like racial, cultural, and national superiority and toward a more inclusive vision of humanity. As people begin to embrace the idea that they are part of a global community, they are more likely to support policies and initiatives that promote cooperation, sustainability, and shared responsibility. In this way, grassroots movements can serve as the catalysts for a cultural transformation that prioritizes human identity over cultural or national allegiances.

In the fight for global citizenship, the role of grassroots movements cannot be overstated. These movements must serve as the engine of change, pushing societies to reimagine what it means to belong to a global community. By organizing locally and globally, grassroots movements have the potential to reshape the political landscape, challenge outdated ideologies, and build a world where cooperation and shared responsibility are the cornerstones of human progress. As the Fridays for Future movement and many others have shown, grassroots activism is not just about addressing immediate concerns—it is about laying the foundation for a future where global citizenship is the norm, and where humanity works together for the common good.

3. Radical Solutions for Global Change

In cases where governments resist global citizenship or promote nationalism and exclusion, more radical solutions may be necessary. Civil disobedience, mass mobilization, and new global governance systems must be considered to break down the barriers of nationalism and cultural identity.

Example: The anti-apartheid movement in South Africa, led by figures like Nelson Mandela and Desmond Tutu, used civil disobedience and international pressure to dismantle the racist apartheid regime. This movement shows how grassroots activism, combined with international solidarity, can challenge and ultimately defeat oppressive systems of division.

4. Call to Action

Global citizenship offers a revolutionary way forward—a new identity that transcends the artificial and destructive divisions of culture, race, religion, and nationality. It is a vision of humanity as one interconnected and interdependent species, where our shared existence on this planet takes precedence over the superficial differences that have historically separated us. By embracing this identity, we unlock the potential for a future defined by peace, prosperity, and unity, rather than conflict, inequality, and division. This shift in how we define ourselves is not just a philosophical concept; it is a radical transformation in how we view our role in the world and our relationship with each other. Global citizenship challenges the very foundations of the existing social, political, and economic systems, offering a path to a future where humanity thrives together.

At its core, global citizenship is about recognizing that the human race is our primary identity. It is a call to move beyond the narrow, exclusionary definitions of self that have been dictated by the accident of birth—whether that birth placed us within a certain nation, culture, or ethnic group. These identities, while once useful for fostering a sense of belonging within small, isolated communities, have become barriers to progress in an interconnected world. In a time when the pressing challenges we face—climate change, global inequality, pandemics, and geopolitical instability—affect every person on the planet, it is clear that the old divisions no longer serve us. Instead, they hold us back, perpetuating cycles of conflict, mistrust, and exploitation.

Global citizenship calls for a fundamental reorientation of our values and priorities. It asks us to place the well-being of humanity as a whole above the interests of individual nations or cultural groups. This does not mean abandoning our personal histories, but it does mean recognizing that the future of humanity depends on our ability to transcend the boundaries that have traditionally defined us. It is about seeing ourselves not just as citizens of a particular country, but as stewards of the Earth—responsible for the health and well-being of the planet and all of its inhabitants.

The potential of global citizenship lies in its ability to unite humanity around common goals. When we embrace this identity, we begin to see that the problems we face are not confined to any one region or group—they are global challenges that require global solutions. Climate change, for example, does not respect national borders. Rising sea levels, extreme weather events, and ecosystem collapse will affect us all, regardless of where we live. By embracing global citizenship, we acknowledge that the survival of humanity depends on our ability to work together to protect the environment and preserve the natural resources that sustain us. No single nation can solve this crisis alone—it will take coordinated action on a global scale, with every person, community, and government working together to mitigate the effects of climate change and build a sustainable future.

Global inequality is another issue that demands a global response. The current system, in which wealth and resources are concentrated in a few countries or within the hands of a select few individuals, perpetuates a world of stark inequities. Billions of people live in poverty, without access to clean water, healthcare, education, or basic human rights, while others enjoy extreme wealth and privilege. This inequality breeds instability, resentment, and conflict, as those who are excluded from the benefits of the global economy are left to struggle for survival. Global citizenship offers a way to address these inequalities by promoting policies that ensure fair distribution of resources and opportunities. It is about recognizing that a world in which some people thrive at the expense of others is unsustainable. By embracing global citizenship, we commit to eradicating poverty, reducing inequality, and ensuring that everyone has access to the resources they need to live with dignity.

At the heart of global citizenship is a radical reimagining of what it means to be human. It is a shift away from the competitive, hierarchical systems that have dominated human society for centuries—systems that prioritize domination, control, and accumulation of power. Instead, global citizenship is built on the principles of cooperation, empathy, and shared responsibility. It is about recognizing that our fates are intertwined, and that the success of one group cannot come at the expense of others. This mindset opens the door to a world where we no longer view others as competitors or threats, but as partners in the collective project of building a just, equitable, and sustainable future.

The path to achieving this vision will not be easy. Embracing global citizenship requires us to confront the entrenched systems of power that are deeply invested in maintaining the status quo. Nationalism, cultural superiority, and economic exploitation have been deeply ingrained in the global order for centuries, and those who benefit from these systems will resist any attempts to dismantle them. But history has shown us that radical change is possible, especially when it is driven by the people. Grassroots movements, activism, and collective action have the power to challenge and overturn oppressive systems. The fight for global citizenship will require a similar effort—a movement that transcends borders and unites people from all walks of life in the pursuit of a more just and compassionate world.

One of the most powerful aspects of global citizenship is its ability to inspire action. When people begin to see themselves as part of a global community, they are more likely to take action on behalf of others, even if those others live far away or are from different cultural backgrounds. This sense of shared responsibility can drive people to mobilize, to demand policies that prioritize the common good over narrow national interests, and to push for radical change when necessary. Global citizens are not passive observers—they are active participants in shaping the future of humanity. They understand that the challenges we face are urgent and existential, and they are willing to take bold action to address them.

Radical change, when necessary, must be pursued with a clear vision of what we hope to achieve. Global citizenship is not about incremental reforms or small adjustments to the existing system—it is about transforming the way we organize society, govern ourselves, and interact with each other and the planet. This may require bold policy changes, such as creating new global institutions that can enforce environmental protections, promote human rights, and ensure fair distribution of resources. It may require civil disobedience, protest, and other forms of activism to demand that leaders take meaningful action on climate change, inequality, and other global crises. And in some cases, it may require radical shifts in the way we think about governance, moving toward a system of global cooperation that transcends the limitations of the nation-state.

A world where global citizenship is the norm is a world where peace, prosperity, and unity are not just ideals, but lived realities. In this world, people are no longer divided by artificial boundaries, but united by their common humanity. Wars, once fought over territory, resources, or ideology, become a thing of the past, as the shared interests of humanity take precedence over narrow political goals. Poverty and inequality are drastically reduced, as resources are distributed equitably and everyone has access to the basic necessities of life. Environmental destruction is halted and reversed, as humanity recognizes its responsibility to protect the planet for future generations.

In this future, the potential for human achievement is limitless. Freed from the constraints of competition and conflict, humanity can focus its energy on innovation, creativity, and progress. Scientific advancements, technological breakthroughs, and artistic expression flourish, driven by a collective desire to improve the human condition. The resources that were once wasted on war, environmental degradation, and exploitation are redirected toward projects that benefit all of humanity—curing diseases, building sustainable cities, exploring the universe, and creating systems that ensure human flourishing.

Ultimately, global citizenship offers a way forward —a path to a future where humanity can overcome the divisions of the past and build a world where everyone can thrive. It is a call to action, inviting us to embrace our shared identity as human beings and to work together for the common good. By embracing global citizenship, we commit to creating a world where peace, prosperity, and unity are not just possibilities, but realities for all of humanity. This is the future we can achieve, but it requires courage, vision, and a willingness to push for radical change when necessary. The time to act is now, and the stakes could not be higher.

Global Leadership and Cooperation: The Role of International Institutions

1. Reforming Global Institutions

Global institutions such as the United Nations, the World Health Organization, and the International Monetary Fund must undergo significant reforms to better reflect the interests of human identity over narrow national interests. For too long, these organizations have been constrained by the political agendas of individual member states, leading to inaction in times of crisis and an inability to address the root causes of global challenges such as climate change, pandemics, and economic inequality. By prioritizing a shared human identity, these institutions can evolve to meet the needs of a globalized world, where collective action is necessary to solve problems that no single country can manage alone.

These institutions were originally founded with the intention of fostering international cooperation, yet they have often been hampered by the limitations imposed by the nation-state system. The principle of national sovereignty—while historically important —has sometimes prevented timely intervention in humanitarian crises and allowed powerful countries to shape global policies to their own advantage. In a reformed world order, the focus must shift toward global cooperation, with institutions working for the benefit of all people, regardless of nationality, ethnicity, or cultural background.

One of the most prominent examples of the need for reform is the United Nations. While the UN has been successful in many areas—such as peacekeeping, humanitarian aid, and promoting human rights—it has also been criticized for its failures, particularly when it comes to preventing genocides and large-scale atrocities. One tragic example is the Rwandan Genocide of 1994. Despite clear warning signs and evidence of escalating violence, the UN was unable to mobilize a timely response, largely due to the reluctance of certain member states to intervene. This failure highlighted the limitations of an institution that places too much emphasis on national sovereignty and not enough on human life.

A reformed UN would prioritize human identity over national interests, ensuring that the protection of human life takes precedence over political concerns. In this new framework, the UN would have the authority and the resources to intervene swiftly in situations where human rights are at risk, regardless of the political sensitivities involved. The Security Council, in particular, would need to be restructured to reduce the influence of the veto power, which has often been used to block critical interventions due to the interests of a single member state. Instead, decisions would be based on the collective will of humanity, with an emphasis on preventing suffering and promoting peace.

Global institutions also play a vital role in addressing long-term challenges that require sustained international cooperation. Climate change, for instance, is a global crisis that cannot be solved by individual nations acting in isolation. A reformed UN, working in tandem with other international organizations, would lead global efforts to reduce carbon emissions, transition to renewable energy, and protect vulnerable populations from the impacts of environmental degradation. Similarly, in the wake of the COVID-19 pandemic, the need for stronger global health institutions has become clear. By reforming the World Health Organization and creating new frameworks for international cooperation on public health, we can ensure that future pandemics are dealt with swiftly and effectively, without the delays and political interference that have plagued past responses.

Furthermore, global institutions must take a leading role in addressing economic inequality, which continues to be a driving force behind instability, conflict, and environmental degradation. The current global economic system has resulted in vast disparities in wealth and opportunity, both within and between countries. Institutions such as the International Monetary Fund and the World Bank need to be reformed to prioritize equitable development and the fair distribution of resources, rather than simply promoting the interests of the wealthiest nations. A reformed system would focus on lifting all people out of poverty, promoting sustainable economic practices, and ensuring that the benefits of global economic growth are shared by all.

In summary, the reform of global institutions is not only necessary but urgent. These institutions, with their potential to bring together the global community, must evolve to reflect a world where human identity takes precedence over narrow national interests. By doing so, they can lead the charge in addressing the global challenges of our time—whether it be preventing future atrocities, mitigating climate change, or reducing economic inequality. Only through cooperative global action can we create a future where all people are able to live in peace, prosperity, and dignity.

2. International Cooperation for Global Challenges

Global cooperation is not just important—it is absolutely essential for addressing the challenges that transcend national borders, such as climate change, pandemics, economic inequality, and environmental degradation. These global issues do not respect the arbitrary boundaries of nations or political borders, nor can they be solved by any one country acting in isolation. To combat these crises effectively, the world must come together to form united, cohesive strategies that reflect a collective commitment to the well-being of the entire human race and the planet we share.

The interdependence of nations has never been clearer than in today's globalized world, where the actions of one country can have profound consequences for the rest of the planet. Climate change is perhaps the most obvious example. Carbon emissions from industrial activity, deforestation, and other human activities affect the entire Earth's climate system, causing extreme weather events, rising sea levels, and shifts in ecosystems that threaten the lives and livelihoods of millions of people. Addressing climate change requires a coordinated global effort in which every nation is committed to reducing emissions, transitioning to sustainable energy sources, and protecting vulnerable ecosystems. No country can solve climate change on its own because the atmosphere does not respect national borders—every country must contribute to the solution.

The Paris Agreement of 2015 is a powerful

example of international cooperation on climate change. Signed by nearly every nation in the world, the agreement marked a historic moment of collective action, where governments pledged to limit global warming to well below 2°C above pre-industrial levels, with the aim of limiting it to 1.5°C. The agreement represents a global consensus that climate change is a shared challenge requiring immediate and sustained action. It also highlights the potential for international cooperation to achieve ambitious goals when nations come together to address common threats. However, the withdrawal of some nations—most notably the United States in 2017 under the Trump administration—revealed the fragility of such agreements when national interests conflict with global efforts. The U.S. withdrawal undermined the progress of the Paris Agreement and weakened the global response to climate change, illustrating how the pursuit of short-term national gains can jeopardize long-term global goals.

This example underscores the need for global citizenship, which prioritizes the collective good over individual national interests. Under a system of global citizenship, nations would not be able to withdraw from their commitments to the planet or to humanity simply because it is politically expedient or economically advantageous in the short term. Instead, global citizens would recognize that their actions affect the entire world and that the well-being of future generations depends on the collective efforts of all nations today. Global citizenship would ensure that commitments to climate action are upheld by all nations, regardless of shifting political winds or economic pressures, because the health of the planet is a responsibility shared by all.

The challenges posed by pandemics also highlight the critical importance of global cooperation. The COVID-19 pandemic was a stark reminder that diseases do not respect borders, and that an outbreak in one country can quickly spread to every corner of the globe. Early in the pandemic, the lack of coordination between nations led to delays in the global response, with countries competing for medical supplies, closing borders, and prioritizing national interests over collective action. Had there been stronger global cooperation and more robust international frameworks for pandemic preparedness, the world might have been better equipped to manage the crisis, prevent widespread loss of life, and mitigate the economic fallout.

Global cooperation in health is not a new concept; organizations like the World Health Organization (WHO) exist to facilitate coordinated responses to health crises. However, the limitations of such institutions were exposed during the COVID-19 pandemic, as political interference, funding shortfalls, and fragmented responses hampered the ability to contain the virus. In a world where global citizenship is the guiding principle, the international community would work together to strengthen institutions like the WHO, ensuring that every country contributes to the global health system and that resources, information, and vaccines are shared equitably across all regions. This would not only help prevent future pandemics but also ensure that the global health system is robust enough to respond quickly and effectively when they do occur.

Economic inequality, too, cannot be addressed by individual nations acting alone. The global economy is interconnected, with the actions of wealthy nations often having a profound impact on poorer regions. In a world of global citizenship, the focus would be on reducing inequality by promoting fair trade, sustainable development, and the equitable distribution of resources. Countries would work together to ensure that no one is left behind, that all people have access to the resources they need to thrive, and that economic growth benefits the many, not just the few.

In this future, global cooperation would be the norm, and nations would no longer be driven by short-term national interests that undermine the long-term survival of humanity. Instead, leaders and citizens alike would understand that true progress comes from working together, from recognizing that the challenges we face are shared, and from prioritizing human identity over national boundaries. In this world, global institutions like the United Nations, the World Health Organization, and other international bodies would be empowered to act decisively and equitably in the interests of all people, ensuring that the global challenges of the 21st century are met with collective resolve and cooperation.

Global citizenship is the key to unlocking this future. It is the recognition that we are all part of the same global community, and that our fate as a species depends on our ability to work together to solve the problems that transcend borders. By embracing global citizenship, we can ensure that commitments to climate action, pandemic preparedness, and economic justice are upheld by all nations, creating a world where cooperation, not competition, is the driving force behind human progress.

The Role of Grassroots Movements and Civil Disobedience

1. Grassroots Movements in History

Throughout history, grassroots movements have played a pivotal role in driving profound social and political changes, often challenging deeply entrenched systems of oppression. These movements are typically fueled by collective action and the shared desire for justice, equality, and freedom. A notable example is the Civil Rights Movement in the United States, which was spearheaded by figures like Martin Luther King Jr. to end racial segregation and discrimination. Similarly, India's independence movement, led by Mahatma Gandhi, used nonviolent resistance to challenge British colonial rule, inspiring change through civil disobedience and peaceful protest.

These movements demonstrate that nonviolent resistance can serve as a powerful force in confronting and dismantling systems of oppression. In the case of the Civil Rights Movement, decades of legalized racial inequality were confronted through boycotts, marches, and sit-ins, ultimately leading to transformative changes in U.S. law, including the Civil Rights Act of 1964 and the Voting Rights Act of 1965. Likewise, Gandhi's philosophy of Satyagraha, or truth and nonviolent resistance, galvanized millions of Indians to demand independence from British colonialism, resulting in India achieving its freedom in 1947.

These movements also illustrate the power of grassroots activism in galvanizing ordinary people to fight for their rights. Both the Civil Rights Movement and India's independence movement relied not just on the leadership of iconic figures but on the participation of ordinary citizens— students, workers, and activists—who believed in the cause of justice. Their determination to confront injustice through peaceful means laid the foundation for lasting changes in their respective societies, proving that grassroots movements, when driven by principles of nonviolence and persistence, can overcome even the most entrenched systems of power and create enduring social change.

2. When Civil Disobedience Becomes Necessary

In situations where governments resist the principles of global citizenship, the use of civil disobedience may become necessary to challenge oppressive regimes and force meaningful change. When governments prioritize national interests or oppressive systems over the collective good, civil disobedience allows citizens to express dissent in a nonviolent but powerful way. It has been proven throughout history to be an effective tool for confronting unjust laws and systems, especially when other forms of democratic engagement are suppressed or ignored. Civil disobedience not only disrupts the status quo but also brings attention to the injustices that governments or those in power seek to maintain.

One of the most striking examples of civil disobedience in action is the anti-apartheid movement in South Africa. For decades, South Africa was ruled by a racist and oppressive system of apartheid, which legally enforced segregation and discrimination based on race. Black South Africans were denied basic human rights and were forced to live in a state of systemic oppression, all while the government maintained a firm grip on power. However, through civil disobedience, organized protests, and strikes, the anti-apartheid movement, led by figures like Nelson Mandela, brought global attention to the atrocities committed under apartheid. These efforts, combined with international pressure, economic sanctions, and boycotts, eventually led to the dismantling of apartheid and the establishment of a democratic South Africa.

The anti-apartheid movement is a powerful example of how grassroots activism, combined with civil disobedience, can challenge even the most entrenched and oppressive systems. It also demonstrates the potential of the global community to exert pressure on governments that resist progressive change. While the apartheid regime initially resisted reform, the persistent actions of activists, both within and outside South Africa, eventually forced the government to recognize the illegitimacy of its policies. This movement exemplifies how civil disobedience, alongside global solidarity, can achieve monumental change and create a more just and equitable society.

In the context of global citizenship, civil disobedience can be used to challenge governments that resist cooperation on global issues such as climate change, human rights, or economic inequality. When leaders prioritize nationalistic or authoritarian interests over the welfare of humanity as a whole, grassroots movements can step in to confront these injustices through nonviolent resistance. Just as the anti-apartheid movement helped dismantle a system of racial oppression, civil disobedience today can be used to address the global crises that threaten the well-being of humanity and the planet.

Civil disobedience, in the framework of promoting global citizenship, can take various forms—from peaceful protests and sit-ins to boycotts and international campaigns aimed at exposing the failures of governments to act in the interest of the global community. These actions create pressure points, forcing governments to reconsider their policies and pushing for a realignment of national priorities with global interests. In cases where governments refuse to take responsibility for global challenges, such as environmental destruction or human rights abuses, civil disobedience becomes a necessary tool to confront these issues head-on.

Global citizenship demands accountability from governments, and civil disobedience provides a way to hold leaders to account when traditional political processes fail to deliver. When dialogue and negotiation are no longer sufficient, and when governments place national or economic interests above the common good, civil disobedience empowers citizens to stand up for the collective rights of humanity. It is a reminder that power ultimately rests with the people and that, through collective action, it is possible to bring about meaningful change, even in the face of resistance.

Global Crises as Catalysts for Change

Global challenges, such as climate change, pandemics, and economic inequality, are increasingly highlighting the limitations of national identity and borders. These crises transcend geographic boundaries, showing that no country can tackle them in isolation. The scale and complexity of these challenges force the world to reconsider traditional systems based on national sovereignty, as the interconnected nature of global problems requires collective action. National borders, once considered vital for security and identity, are proving inadequate in addressing issues that require global cooperation and shared responsibility.

1. Climate Change as a Unifier

The Pacific Island Nations, including countries like Tuvalu, Kiribati, and the Marshall Islands, face an existential threat from rising sea levels caused by climate change. These small island nations have become some of the most vocal advocates for global climate action, urging the international community to take immediate steps to reduce carbon emissions and protect vulnerable populations. Their plight serves as a stark reminder that climate change is not an issue that can be tackled by individual nations alone. Even though these countries contribute very little to global emissions, they are on the front lines of the climate crisis, with entire communities at risk of displacement due to rising waters. The Pacific Island Nations' calls for cooperation highlight the fact that climate change is a global problem that demands global solutions. It underscores the need for collective responsibility and action, as no single nation, regardless of its size or power, can address the crisis in isolation. The fate of these island nations emphasizes the importance of international cooperation and the moral obligation of wealthier, high-emitting countries to support efforts in mitigating climate impacts and adapting to the consequences.

2. Pandemics and Global Health Crises

The COVID-19 pandemic revealed the critical importance of international cooperation in managing global health crises. The rapid spread of the virus across borders showed that no country, regardless of its wealth or resources, could contain the outbreak alone. The pandemic highlighted the need for collective action to share resources, information, and strategies to combat the virus effectively. Initiatives like COVAX, which aimed to distribute vaccines equitably across the globe, were essential in promoting access to life-saving vaccines for low- and middle-income countries. However, while COVAX represented a vital step toward ensuring vaccine equity, it also revealed the challenges of global health cooperation, as wealthier nations hoarded vaccines, leaving vulnerable populations in developing countries behind.

This experience underscores the necessity of adopting a global citizenship approach to public health, where the focus shifts from national interests to the well-being of all humanity. Under a framework of global citizenship, wealthier nations would recognize their moral responsibility to support global health initiatives, ensuring that vaccines, treatments, and healthcare infrastructure are distributed fairly, regardless of borders. By promoting international solidarity, the world can be better prepared for future pandemics, ensuring that no country is left behind in the response. The COVID-19 pandemic serves as a stark reminder that public health is a shared responsibility and that only through global cooperation can we effectively manage and mitigate the impacts of health crises on a global scale.

Global Citizenship in Practice

Global citizenship is a concept that transcends national borders and asks individuals and communities to recognize their roles in shaping the well-being of the global community. It is not just about large-scale activism but also about the everyday actions that promote empathy, sustainability, and cooperation. Global citizenship can be practiced on both the individual and community levels, where each person and collective plays a critical role in building a more connected and just world. By focusing on local actions that have global implications, individuals and communities can foster a mindset that prioritizes the health of humanity and the planet as a whole.

Addressing Common Criticisms
1. "We'll Lose Our Cultural Identity"
Yes, embracing a shared human identity requires letting go of cultural identities, but this should not be seen as a loss—it's a transformation. Cultural identities have historically divided us, often leading to conflict, prejudice, and exclusion. By discarding these divisions, we free ourselves from the boundaries that hold humanity back. A human identity unites us through shared values like cooperation, empathy, and collective responsibility. It allows us to focus on the common good, ensuring the survival and flourishing of all people, rather than being tied to outdated cultural divisions.

2. "Global Governance Undermines National Sovereignty"
Global governance does require a surrender of national sovereignty, but this sacrifice is essential for addressing the global challenges—such as climate change and pandemics—that no nation can resolve alone. In this new system, the interests of humanity take precedence over national borders and sovereignty. By adopting global governance, we

ensure that decisions are made for the collective well-being of all people, prioritizing the survival and prosperity of the human race rather than the self-interest of individual nations.

A Vision for the Future

Imagine a world where borders are no longer barriers—where they exist only in history books as reminders of a time when humanity was divided by artificial lines. In this future, people are no longer defined by their nationality, ethnicity, or culture. Instead, they identify as members of the human race, united in a shared purpose and responsibility. The world has embraced the idea of human identity, recognizing that our differences are superficial and that the survival and prosperity of our species depend on unity.

The Freedom to Live Without Borders

In this future, migration is no longer an issue of nationality or ethnicity. People move freely across the planet, not because they are forced by conflict or poverty, but because they are driven by a shared desire to improve the human condition. No longer confined by outdated concepts of cultural identity, individuals work and live wherever their skills and passions are most needed.

Borders, once guarded with hostility, are now relics of the past. The world has evolved beyond the limitations of national pride and cultural heritage.

People see themselves as citizens of Earth, their goals aligned with the betterment of humanity as a whole. This shift has created unprecedented levels of collaboration and cooperation across the globe, as human beings come together to solve common challenges and build a shared future.

Global Cooperation for Shared Solutions

Nations, as they were once known, no longer see themselves as isolated actors vying for power and dominance on the world stage. The zero-sum mentality that once defined international relations —where one nation's gain was seen as another's loss—has been replaced by the understanding that the well-being of any individual or community is inseparably tied to the well-being of all. With the emergence of a unified global government, the world is guided by the principle that the challenges facing humanity are too vast and interconnected to be solved by isolated entities. The concept of fragmented nations, each pursuing its own agenda, has become a relic of the past, replaced by a single governing body committed to the prosperity and sustainability of the entire human race.

Gone are the days when different regions or cultures competed for resources, power, and influence. The fierce competition for control over oil reserves, land, and other valuable resources—conflicts that fueled many of the wars and crises in human history —has been replaced by a cooperative approach to managing the planet's resources. The old paradigms of scarcity and hoarding, driven by nationalistic or economic self-interest, have been discarded, replaced by the understanding that sharing resources is not just a moral imperative but a practical necessity for the survival and flourishing of humanity. People no longer see themselves as part of rival factions but as members of one human community, united by a shared responsibility to protect and sustain the Earth for future generations.

The conflicts of the past, which were so often rooted in cultural, national, or religious divisions, are now viewed as tragic mistakes—cautionary tales of what happens when humanity is divided by superficial differences. The territorial disputes, proxy wars, and ideological battles that once defined global relations have given way to a new era of unified governance, where cooperation and shared responsibility are the driving forces behind every decision. The unified global government focuses not on maintaining power or securing regional interests but on addressing the global challenges that transcend borders—such as climate change, environmental degradation, poverty, and pandemics. These challenges are no longer seen as issues for individual countries to handle but as collective challenges requiring coordinated global action.

In this future, the driving force behind every

decision is a profound sense of shared responsibility. The unified government understands that every action—whether related to environmental policy, economic development, or social reform—has global consequences. It recognizes that a polluted river in one area can affect ecosystems and communities far downstream, that economic inequality in one region can destabilize the entire global economy, and that a disease outbreak in a remote village can quickly spread across continents. This deep understanding of interconnectedness has transformed decision-making, shifting the focus from short-term regional interests to long-term global well-being.

Take, for example, the once-looming existential threat of climate change. In the past, countries bickered over who should bear the responsibility for reducing greenhouse gas emissions, with wealthier nations blaming developing countries, and vice versa. These disagreements often led to inaction, allowing the planet's environmental health to deteriorate. But under the unified global government, climate change is no longer seen as a problem to be negotiated between conflicting national interests—it is recognized as a global challenge that requires collective action. The unified government has implemented comprehensive policies to restore the planet's health and ensure the sustainability of natural resources for all people.

Former competitors in the fossil fuel industry—

regions that once fought for control over oil reserves and energy markets—are now leading the charge in the development of renewable energy technologies. Solar, wind, geothermal, and other clean energy sources power the entire world, providing affordable, sustainable energy to even the most remote areas. The once-powerful fossil fuel industries have been transformed into pioneers of the clean energy revolution, creating a global infrastructure that is sustainable, equitable, and accessible to all. The profits generated by this new energy economy are no longer concentrated in the hands of a few, but are reinvested into communities, helping to lift people out of poverty and creating new opportunities for economic and social development.

The Earth's resources, once hoarded by powerful nations or monopolized by corporations, are now shared freely under the stewardship of the unified government. Access to clean water, nutritious food, shelter, and energy is recognized as a basic human right for all, not as privileges reserved for the wealthy or powerful. In this new era of abundance and sustainability, the concept of competing for finite resources is a thing of the past. Instead of fighting over who gets the largest share, humanity has embraced the idea that cooperation is the only way to ensure that everyone's needs are met and that the planet's ecosystems are preserved.

The unified government's global environmental

initiative has also led to the restoration of ecosystems that were once on the brink of collapse. Rainforests, which were once clear-cut for agriculture or development, have been replanted and protected, becoming thriving ecosystems once again. Oceans, once choked with plastic pollution and overfished to the point of collapse, are now carefully managed, with strict protections in place to ensure the health of marine life. Endangered species, which were once driven to the brink of extinction, are now flourishing thanks to coordinated conservation efforts that span continents and ecosystems.

In this new era of unified global governance, the fates of all people are recognized as interconnected. No longer do regions pursue self-serving policies at the expense of global stability. Instead, the unified government prioritizes the collective good, recognizing that the health and prosperity of one community are inseparable from the health and prosperity of the world as a whole. This shift has transformed the dynamics of international relations, replacing fear, distrust, and competition with trust, respect, and mutual support.

The economic inequality that once drove global instability and conflict has been addressed through a combination of redistributive policies, fair trade practices, and international development programs. Wealth is no longer concentrated in the hands of a select few; instead, the global economy ensures that resources are distributed equitably, allowing every community to share in the benefits of growth and development. Economic systems are no longer driven by profit maximization or exploitation but are based on the principles of sustainability, fairness, and shared prosperity.

In this future, education, healthcare, and clean energy are not luxuries reserved for the elite but basic human rights available to all. The unified government has created a global framework to ensure that every child has access to a quality education, that everyone can receive the medical care they need, and that every home is powered by clean, renewable energy. These advancements have transformed the quality of life for billions of people, creating a world where no one is left behind.

The era of competition and conflict has given way to an era of collaboration and unity. Humanity no longer seeks to dominate or outmaneuver one another; instead, people work together as equal participants in the shared project of building a better future for all. The old divisions of race, religion, and nationality—once sources of division and rivalry—have been transcended, replaced by a shared commitment to human flourishing. This is the world that has been built under a unified global government, where competition for resources and power has been replaced by cooperation, sustainability, and mutual respect.

A Revolution in Technology

Technological advancements have accelerated rapidly as the barriers of national interest and competition have fallen away. Scientists and engineers from all over the globe collaborate openly, sharing knowledge and breakthroughs without the constraints of intellectual property or corporate greed. This has resulted in monumental advances in healthcare, artificial intelligence, and space exploration, all directed toward the common goal of improving the human condition.

Example: Diseases that once ravaged humanity have been eradicated, thanks to global cooperation in medical research. Lifesaving treatments are shared universally, with healthcare no longer determined by wealth or geography. The global pursuit of knowledge has extended beyond Earth's atmosphere, with human missions to Mars and beyond becoming reality. These missions are not for the glory of any one nation but for the advancement of the human race.

A New Era of Global Governance

Global governance has replaced the fragmented and often conflict-driven political systems of the past. A unified global council, representing the interests of all people, ensures that decisions are made in the best interest of humanity as a whole. This system of governance is transparent and inclusive, utilizing advanced technology to ensure that every global citizen has a voice in shaping the future.

Example: The Global Council, composed of representatives chosen for their commitment to human progress rather than their nationality or political affiliations, oversees the implementation of policies that prioritize sustainability, human rights, and global prosperity. Decisions are no longer influenced by cultural biases or national agendas; they are driven by data, ethical considerations, and a commitment to the collective well-being of humanity.

The Elimination of Poverty and Inequality
Economic systems have been restructured to ensure that resources are distributed fairly and that no one is left behind. Wealth is no longer concentrated in the hands of a few nations or individuals. Instead, it is shared globally, based on need and contribution to the collective good. In this world, poverty and hunger have been eliminated, and every human being has access to the basic necessities of life—food, clean water, healthcare, and education.

Example: Rural communities that were once isolated and impoverished now thrive thanks to global investment in infrastructure and innovation. Clean energy, education, and healthcare are accessible to all, and the global economy is built on principles of fairness and sustainability. No longer do people compete for scarce resources; instead, they work together to ensure that everyone benefits from the advancements in technology and industry.

Human Flourishing Without Cultural Divisions

In this future, humanity is no longer divided by the concepts of race, ethnicity, or cultural heritage. These identities, once a source of pride or division, have been replaced by a singular focus on our shared humanity. People no longer look to their past to define who they are; instead, they are motivated by the potential of the human race as a united species.

Art, innovation, and knowledge are driven by a desire to explore the limitless possibilities of human creativity and cooperation. Freed from the constraints of cultural identity, people collaborate across former boundaries to create a better world for all. The barriers that once separated us—whether linguistic, religious, or ethnic—have been dissolved, allowing for true unity and progress.

Example: Imagine a city where people from all backgrounds live side by side, not as representatives of their culture or ethnicity, but as human beings working toward a common goal. They share ideas, create innovations, and contribute to a global society that values every individual for their talents and contributions, not for the identity they were born into. In this world, cultural distinctions have been replaced by a deep sense of connection to the greater human family.

Humanity's Collective Future

The challenges that once seemed insurmountable —war, poverty, environmental destruction, and the countless crises that humanity once faced—are now seen as mere mistakes of the past, relics of an era when division and competition ruled the human psyche. These challenges, which at one time felt like unmovable mountains, have been revealed as obstacles born not from the intrinsic limitations of human nature but from the artificial boundaries and divisions we imposed upon ourselves. Now, in this brighter future, humanity looks back on these errors with the clarity that comes from wisdom and progress. The conflicts and crises that once defined human history are remembered as essential lessons —lessons that had to be learned along the way to create a more united, compassionate, and peaceful world.

In this future, humanity is no longer fragmented by the divisions that once separated us into competing tribes, nations, or religious groups. We have discarded the cultural baggage of the past and embraced a shared identity, one that is not constrained by borders or superficial differences. This is a world where cooperation has replaced competition as the driving force behind human progress. The idea that one nation, group, or individual must succeed at the expense of another is a relic of a bygone era. Instead, people everywhere have come to understand that true progress is only possible when we work together, pooling our collective knowledge, resources, and energy for the common good.

In this future, the driving motivation behind human activity is not personal gain, national pride, or cultural superiority, but a commitment to the survival and flourishing of all people. The well-being of every individual is seen as inseparable from the well-being of humanity as a whole. People no longer define their success by how much they can accumulate for themselves or their immediate community; instead, they measure success by how much they can contribute to the betterment of the human race. This collective mindset has allowed humanity to overcome challenges that once seemed impossible to solve. The problems of war, poverty, and environmental degradation—problems that had plagued us for centuries—are now understood as symptoms of a world divided by artificial boundaries, not as inevitable aspects of the human condition.

War, once a constant presence in human history, has been consigned to the past. The idea that people would take up arms against one another over territorial disputes, religious differences, or ethnic divisions now seems unthinkable. The conflicts that once led to untold suffering and destruction—

World Wars, civil wars, genocides—are remembered as tragic mistakes, born from a time when humanity had not yet embraced its shared identity. In this future, the mechanisms that once fueled war—nationalism, militarism, and the pursuit of dominance—have been dismantled. The resources that were once spent on building armies, stockpiling weapons, and preparing for conflict are now devoted to improving the human condition. In place of military alliances, we have global partnerships dedicated to peace, justice, and human flourishing.

The concept of poverty, too, has been transformed. In this future, the vast inequalities that once defined the global economy have been eradicated. No longer are billions of people trapped in a cycle of deprivation, struggling to meet their basic needs while a small minority controls the vast majority of the world's wealth. Instead, resources are shared equitably, and every person has access to the essentials of life—clean water, nutritious food, healthcare, education, and shelter. The elimination of poverty has not only improved the quality of life for millions of people but has also unleashed the full potential of humanity. With everyone able to contribute to society without the burden of survival weighing them down, human innovation, creativity, and collaboration have reached unprecedented heights.

The environmental devastation that once threatened

the survival of humanity has been reversed through collective action. The reckless exploitation of natural resources, the destruction of ecosystems, and the pollution of the planet—all driven by the short-sighted pursuit of profit and growth—are now recognized as mistakes of the past. In this future, humanity has embraced sustainability as a core value, understanding that the health of the planet is inextricably linked to the survival of our species. The transition to renewable energy is complete, and the destructive reliance on fossil fuels is a distant memory. Forests that were once clear-cut are now thriving ecosystems, oceans that were once choked with plastic are teeming with life, and the air that was once polluted with toxins is now clean and breathable.

This environmental restoration has not only saved the planet from ecological collapse but has also transformed the way humanity interacts with the natural world. People no longer see themselves as separate from or superior to nature; instead, they understand that they are part of a larger, interconnected web of life. This shift in perspective has fostered a deep respect for the environment and a commitment to preserving it for future generations. The global community works together to ensure that the Earth's resources are managed sustainably and that all people have access to the clean air, water, and food they need to thrive.

In this future, human beings are no longer defined by where they come from or what culture they belong to. The divisions of race, ethnicity, religion, and nationality—once so central to human identity—have been replaced by a more profound understanding of what it means to be human. People are no longer labeled or categorized based on the circumstances of their birth. Instead, they are defined by their shared potential, by what they are capable of achieving together. This shift in identity has opened the door to a new era of human cooperation and progress, one in which the artificial divisions of the past no longer hold us back.

The dream of peace, unity, and shared prosperity is no longer a distant hope, something to be longed for but never achieved. It is a living reality—a world where people of all backgrounds work together in harmony, free from the prejudices and divisions that once tore us apart. In this world, the progress of the human race is driven not by competition or conflict, but by a shared commitment to building a future where everyone can thrive. This is a world where technological innovation, scientific discovery, and artistic expression are fueled by the desire to improve the human condition, not by the pursuit of individual or national glory.

The advancements that have been made in science and technology in this future are astounding, and they are made possible by the collaborative efforts of people from every corner of the globe. Scientists, engineers, and innovators work together without the constraints of intellectual property laws or the desire to outcompete one another. Knowledge is shared freely, and the breakthroughs that have been achieved—from curing diseases to creating clean energy solutions—are used to benefit all of humanity, not just a select few. The spirit of cooperation that defines this future has accelerated human progress in ways that were once unimaginable, allowing us to solve problems that had seemed beyond our reach.

This world is also one where art and culture flourish, not as tools for division, but as expressions of our shared humanity. While the cultural identities that once divided us have been transcended, the creative expressions of human experience remain as vibrant as ever. Art, music, literature, and film are used not to reinforce cultural boundaries, but to explore the universal themes that connect us all—love, loss, hope, and the search for meaning. In this future, people from all walks of life come together to celebrate the diversity of human expression, not as a marker of difference, but as a testament to the richness of the human experience.

This is the world that can be built when we embrace our shared human identity. It is a world where the divisions of the past are seen as lessons, not as permanent barriers. It is a world where we have moved beyond the rivalries, conflicts, and prejudices that once held us back and have come to understand that our true potential lies in what we can achieve together. This future is not built on the exclusion of others, nor on the elevation of one group over another, but on the recognition that we are all part of the same human family, united by our common fate.

By moving beyond the divisions that have defined so much of human history, we unlock the potential for true global unity—a unity that is not based on uniformity or conformity, but on mutual respect, understanding, and cooperation. In this future, we are no longer held back by the fears and insecurities that once led us to define ourselves by our differences. Instead, we embrace a more expansive vision of what it means to be human, one that prioritizes the survival and flourishing of all people.

This future is within our reach, but it requires us to make a conscious choice—to let go of the past, to discard the cultural baggage that has weighed us down, and to embrace the possibilities of a new world. It requires us to see each other not as competitors or enemies, but as partners in the great project of building a better future. And most importantly, it requires us to understand that our shared identity as human beings is the most powerful tool we have for overcoming the challenges that lie ahead.

This is the world that awaits us when we embrace our shared human identity and move beyond the divisions that have held us back for so long. It is a world of peace, unity, and shared prosperity, where cooperation and empathy are the driving forces behind human progress. It is a world where every person, regardless of where they come from, is valued for what they can contribute to the collective good, and where the dream of a better future is not just a hope but a reality.

Conclusion

This book is more than just an exploration of ideas —it is a call to action. For far too long, humanity has been divided by artificial boundaries, cultural differences, and the false belief that our identities are rooted in nationality, religion, and ethnicity. These divisions have led to endless cycles of conflict, misunderstanding, and missed opportunities for cooperation. The wars, genocides, and suffering of the past have been fueled by the belief that we are different, that we belong to separate groups, and that those differences justify the walls we build between us.

But as we've seen, this way of thinking is not only outdated—it is dangerous. In an increasingly interconnected world, the challenges we face cannot be solved by isolated nations or communities. Climate change, pandemics, economic inequality, and technological disruption are all problems that transcend borders. They affect every person on this planet, regardless of their race, religion, or the place they were born. And yet, we continue to cling to the idea that these divisions matter more than our shared humanity.

Global citizenship offers a way forward. It is not just an idea—it is a new way of thinking, a radical shift in how we see ourselves and our place in the world. To be a global citizen is to recognize that we are all part of the same species, that our fates are intertwined, and that our survival depends on our ability to work together. It is about replacing the narrow identities we've been taught to cling to with a new identity —one based on the recognition that we are all human, and that our commonalities far outweigh our differences.

This vision of global citizenship isn't just about solving problems—it's about unlocking humanity's full potential. Imagine what we could achieve if we no longer wasted resources on war, on building walls, on dividing people. Imagine if, instead, we focused all our energy on collaboration, on innovation, and on creating a world where every person has the opportunity to thrive. This is not a utopian dream—it is a real possibility, but only if we are willing to make the necessary changes.

The first step toward building this future is to

recognize that the divisions of the past must be left behind. This requires a deep, personal transformation. It means letting go of the identities that have defined us—our culture, our religion, our nationality—and embracing a new identity that is rooted in our shared humanity. This is not easy. It will require many of us to confront feelings of loss, fear, and even betrayal as we let go of the past. But as difficult as it may be, it is the only way forward. The alternative—clinging to the divisions that have caused so much harm—will only lead to more conflict, more suffering, and, ultimately, the potential collapse of human civilization.

The transformation to global citizenship begins with the individual, but it cannot end there. It must spread to communities, nations, and the world. We must build movements that push for change at every level of society. At the local level, we can educate others, organize, and raise awareness about the importance of global citizenship. At the national level, we must hold our leaders accountable, pushing them to adopt policies that promote international cooperation, sustainability, and human rights. And at the global level, we must reform institutions like the United Nations and create new structures of governance that reflect our commitment to human identity rather than national interests.

We cannot rely solely on governments to lead this change. History has shown us that true transformation comes from the grassroots—from ordinary people who are willing to stand up and demand a better world. The Civil Rights Movement, the fight against apartheid, the global climate strikes—all of these movements began with individuals who refused to accept the status quo and who believed that change was possible. Now, it is our turn to take up that mantle and demand a world without borders, without divisions, and without the false identities that have held us back for so long.

As we stand on the brink of an uncertain future, the stakes could not be higher. Climate change threatens the very survival of our species. Pandemics have shown us how vulnerable we are when we fail to cooperate. Economic inequality continues to drive unrest and conflict. And as technology advances, we face new ethical challenges that will require global solutions. If we do not embrace global citizenship now—if we do not work together to solve these problems—humanity's future is at risk.

But if we do—if we rise to the challenge and embrace our shared human identity—the possibilities are limitless. We can create a world where every person has access to clean water, education, and healthcare. A world where poverty is a thing of the past, where every child can grow up without fear of violence or hunger. A world where technological advancements benefit all of humanity, not just a privileged few. A world where we explore the stars, not in the name of any one nation, but in the name of human curiosity and progress.

The vision of global citizenship is not just about survival—it's about flourishing. It's about building a world where humanity can reach its full potential, unburdened by the divisions that have held us back for millennia. It's about creating a society where cooperation, empathy, and compassion are the driving forces behind everything we do.

The future of humanity depends on our ability to transcend the divisions of the past and embrace a new way of thinking. It's time to take action—on a personal, community, and global level. This is the moment when we must decide whether we will cling to the identities of the past or embrace the possibilities of the future. It's time to let go of the things that divide us and focus on the one thing that unites us: our shared identity as human beings.

By embracing global citizenship, we can build a future where humanity not only survives but flourishes. The choice is ours, and the time to act is now.